I0796059

AMERICA THE BEAUTIFUL

WIDE EYED EDITIONS

AMERICA THE BEAUTIFUL
is a song you may have heard in school, at sports games, or during special holidays like the Fourth of July. It's loved for its beautiful words about the mountains, skies, and fields that make up our country. **But did you know it started as a poem?**

In the summer of 1893, a woman named Katharine Lee Bates, who was a college teacher, took a trip from Massachusetts to Colorado. On the way, she saw amazing sights–golden wheat fields, wide open skies, and tall mountain ranges. **When she reached the top of Pikes Peak in Colorado, the view was so breathtaking that she wanted to write down how she felt and what she saw.** The poem became *America the Beautiful.*

Her poem was first printed in a church magazine in 1895, and people loved it.

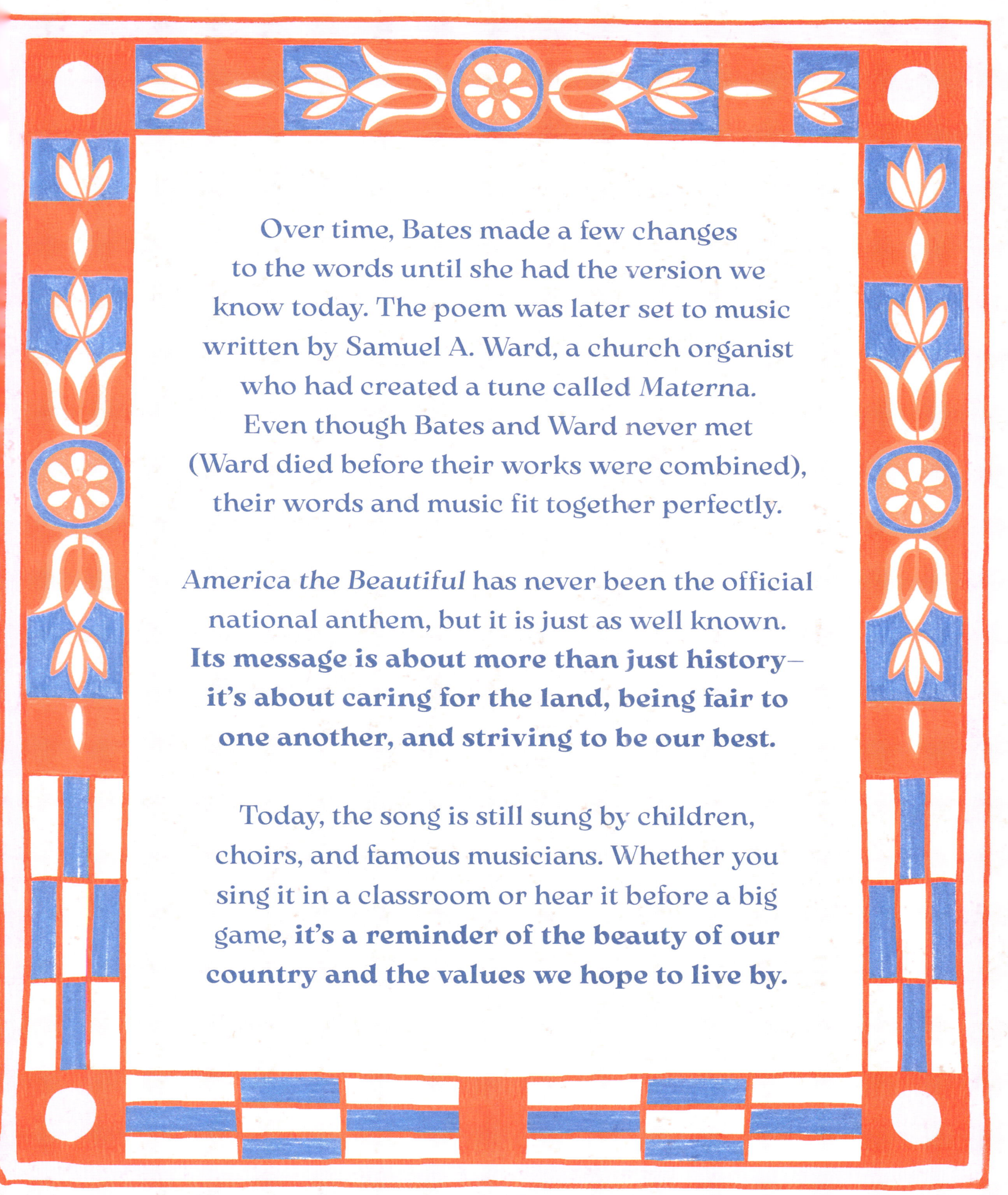

Over time, Bates made a few changes to the words until she had the version we know today. The poem was later set to music written by Samuel A. Ward, a church organist who had created a tune called *Materna.* Even though Bates and Ward never met (Ward died before their works were combined), their words and music fit together perfectly.

America the Beautiful has never been the official national anthem, but it is just as well known. **Its message is about more than just history—it's about caring for the land, being fair to one another, and striving to be our best.**

Today, the song is still sung by children, choirs, and famous musicians. Whether you sing it in a classroom or hear it before a big game, **it's a reminder of the beauty of our country and the values we hope to live by.**

O BEAUTIFUL
FOR
SPACIOUS SKIES,
FOR AMBER
WAVES of GRAIN

For purple mountain majesties
Above the fruited plain!

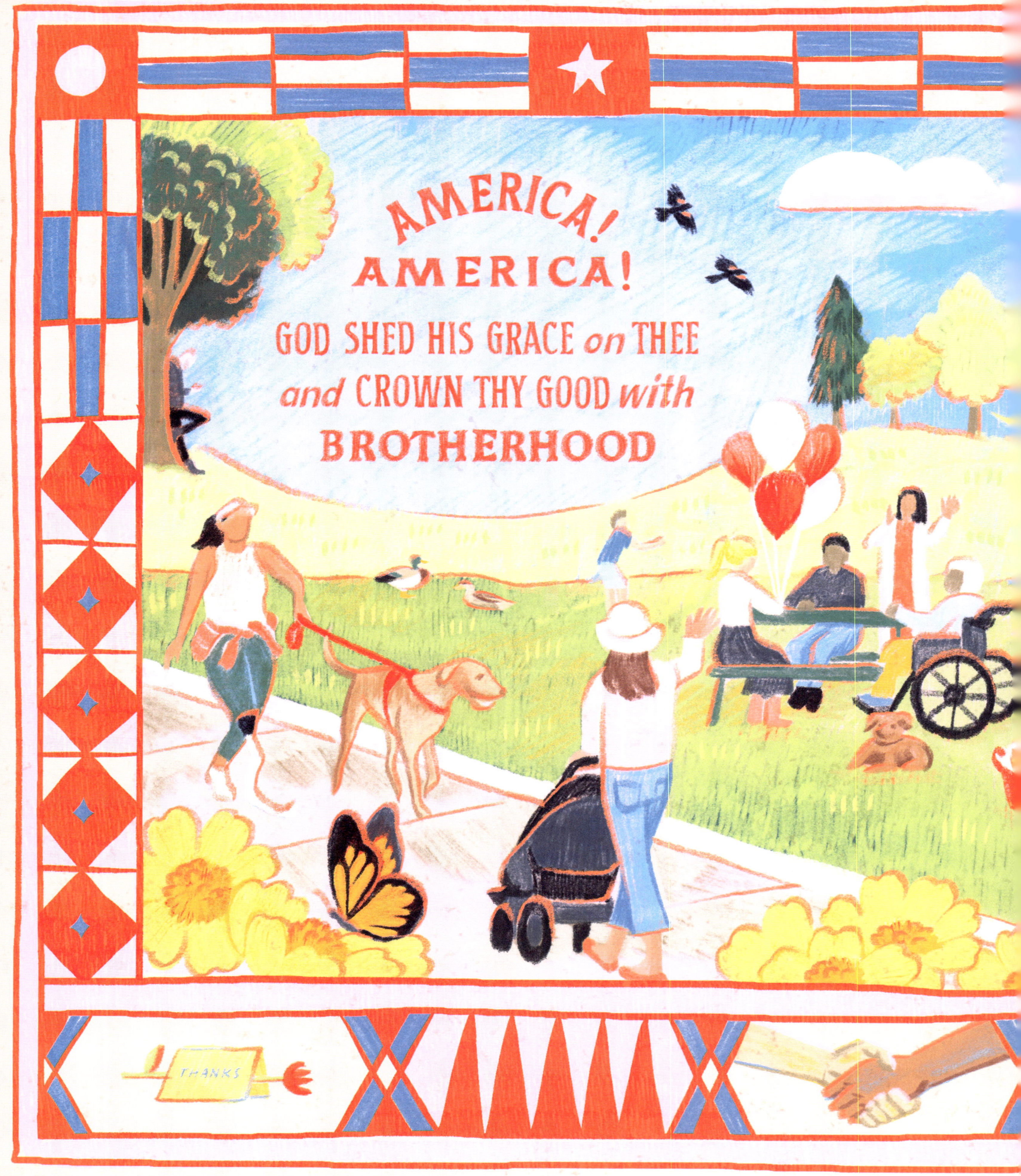

AMERICA!
AMERICA!
GOD SHED HIS GRACE on THEE
and CROWN THY GOOD with
BROTHERHOOD
THANKS

From sea to shining sea!

O beautiful for pilgrim feet,
Whose stern, impassioned stress
A thoroughfare for freedom beat
Across the wilderness!

VOTES
FOR
WOMEN

AMERICA!
AMERICA!
GOD MEND
THINE EVERY
FLAW.

Confirm thy soul in self-control,
Thy liberty in law!

CESAR CHAVEZ
MARSHA P. JOHNSON
RACHEL CARSON
MARTIN LUTHER KING, JR.

O beautiful for heroes proved
In liberating strife,
Who more than self their country loved
And mercy more than life!

AB
E

AMERICA!
AMERICA!
MAY GOD THY GOLD REFINE,
TILL ALL
SUCCESS
BE NOBLENESS,
and EVERY GAIN
DIVINE!

O beautiful for patriot dream
That sees beyond the years

4
Thine alabaster cities gleam
Undimmed by human tears!

COME
ON
IN!

AMERICA!
AMERICA!
GOD SHED HIS GRACE on THEE
and CROWN THY GOOD
with
BROTHERHOOD
OPEN

FROM SEA
TO SHINING
SEA!

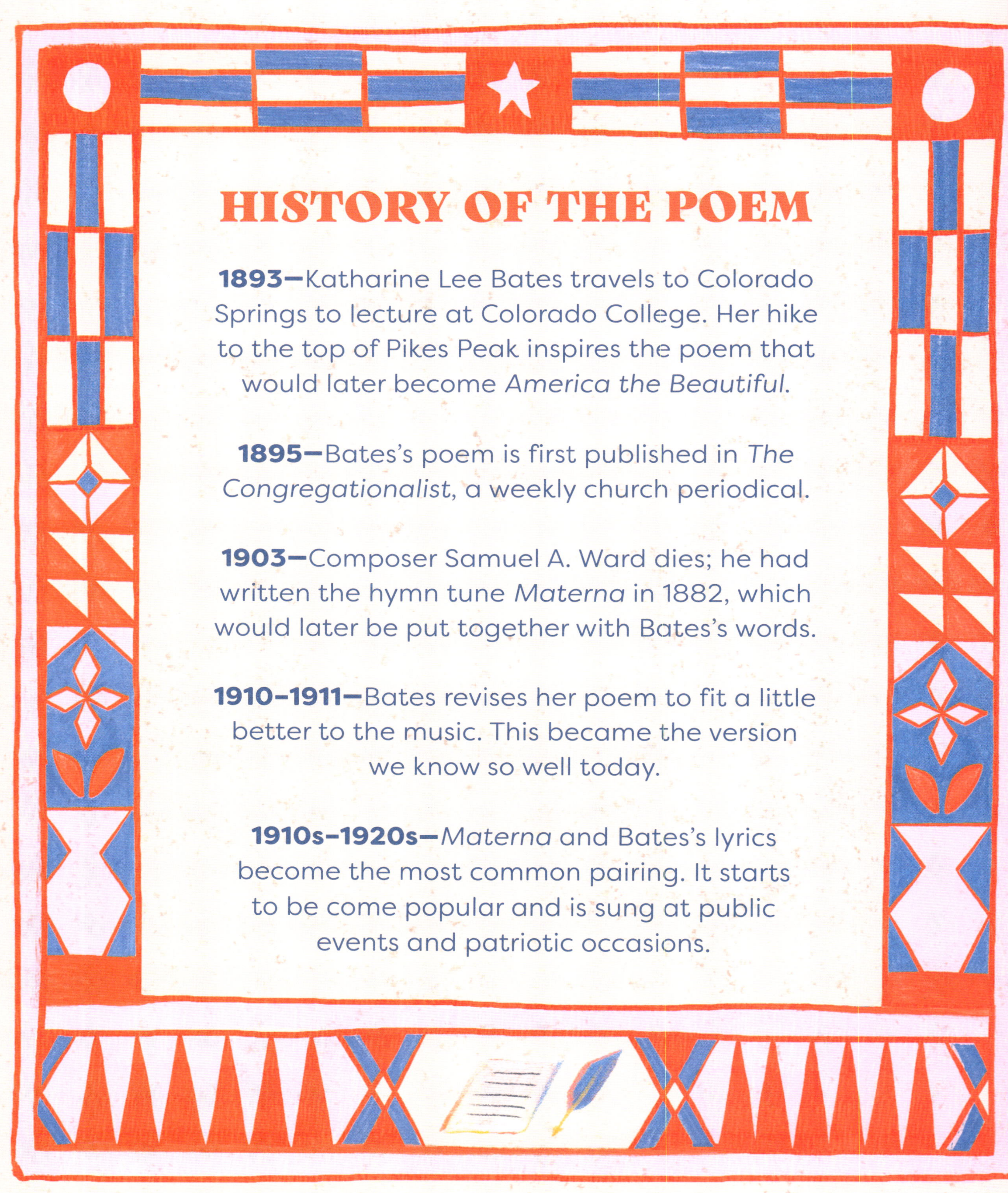

HISTORY OF THE POEM

1893—Katharine Lee Bates travels to Colorado Springs to lecture at Colorado College. Her hike to the top of Pikes Peak inspires the poem that would later become *America the Beautiful*.

1895—Bates's poem is first published in *The Congregationalist*, a weekly church periodical.

1903—Composer Samuel A. Ward dies; he had written the hymn tune *Materna* in 1882, which would later be put together with Bates's words.

1910–1911—Bates revises her poem to fit a little better to the music. This became the version we know so well today.

1910s–1920s—*Materna* and Bates's lyrics become the most common pairing. It starts to be come popular and is sung at public events and patriotic occasions.

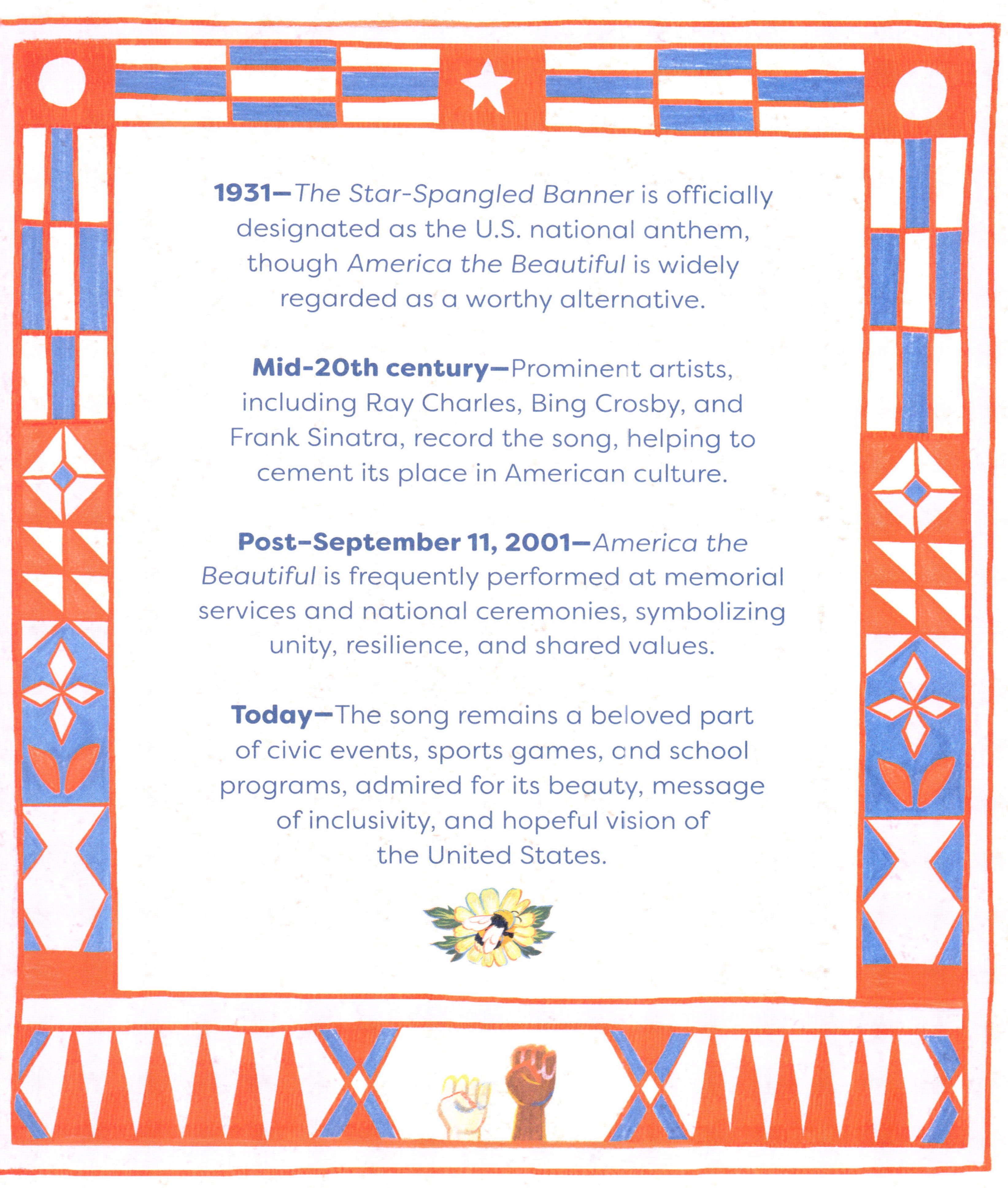

1931—*The Star-Spangled Banner* is officially designated as the U.S. national anthem, though *America the Beautiful* is widely regarded as a worthy alternative.

Mid-20th century—Prominent artists, including Ray Charles, Bing Crosby, and Frank Sinatra, record the song, helping to cement its place in American culture.

Post–September 11, 2001—*America the Beautiful* is frequently performed at memorial services and national ceremonies, symbolizing unity, resilience, and shared values.

Today—The song remains a beloved part of civic events, sports games, and school programs, admired for its beauty, message of inclusivity, and hopeful vision of the United States.

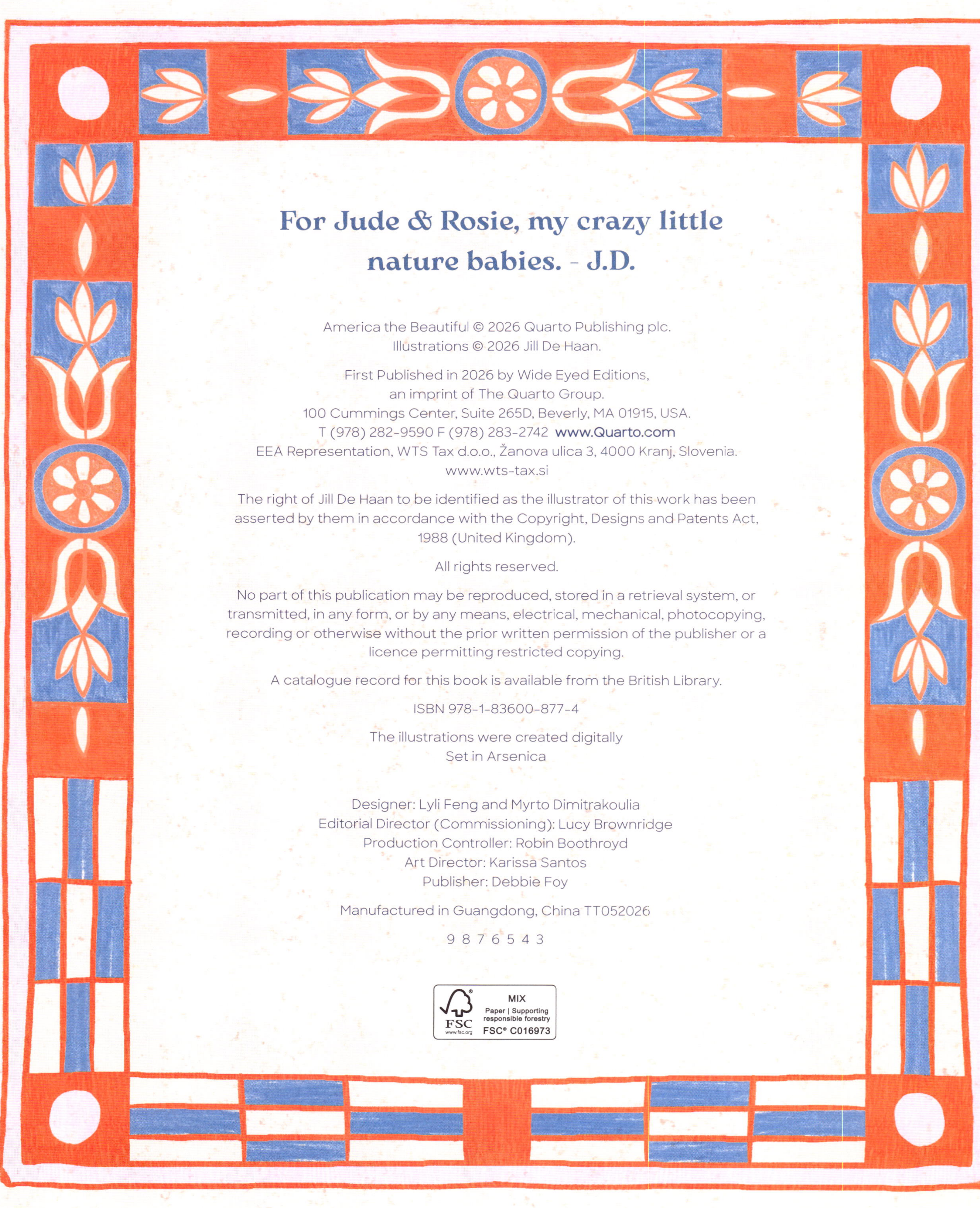

For Jude & Rosie, my crazy little nature babies. - J.D.

First Published in 2026 by Wide Eyed Editions,
an imprint of The Quarto Group.
100 Cummings Center, Suite 265D, Beverly, MA 01915, USA.
T (978) 282-9590 F (978) 283-2742 **www.Quarto.com**
EEA Representation, WTS Tax d.o.o., Žanova ulica 3, 4000 Kranj, Slovenia.
www.wts-tax.si

A catalogue record for this book is available from the British Library.

ISBN 978-1-83600-877-4

The illustrations were created digitally
Set in Arsenica

Designer: Lyli Feng and Myrto Dimitrakoulia
Editorial Director (Commissioning): Lucy Brownridge
Production Controller: Robin Boothroyd
Art Director: Karissa Santos
Publisher: Debbie Foy

Manufactured in Guangdong, China TT052026

9 8 7 6 5 4 3

MIX
Paper | Supporting responsible forestry
FSC® C016973
FSC www.fsc.org